LOVE
ELIXIRS

TITANIA'S BOOK OF ROMANTIC POTIONS

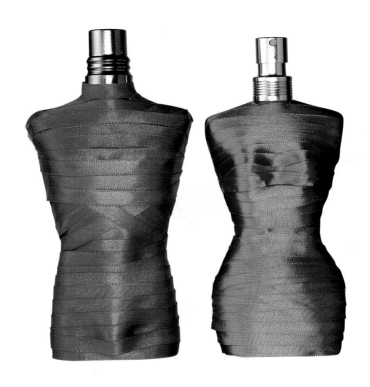

LOVE ELIXIRS

TITANIA'S BOOK OF ROMANTIC POTIONS

TITANIA HARDIE

PHOTOGRAPHS BY SARA MORRIS

CEDCO PUBLISHING

This little volume is especially for Annelise Mary Ebbeck—the goddess of love of my teen years: darling Lisa, where are you now? Also, it is for all those with love in their bosoms: to the witchlings of the world. Keep spreading love and joy and good will, with gentle tolerance for all, and we'll eventually break down centuries of misunderstanding!

"WE'LL TEACH YOU TO DRINK DEEP ERE YOU DEPART!"
Shakespeare, Hamlet

Also by Titania Hardie

SPELLCARDS Health and Happiness

SPELLCARDS Love and Success

TITANIA'S FORTUNE CARDS

WHITE MAGIC

WITCH IN THE KITCHEN
Published by Cedco

An introduction to making love potions ♣

Ben Jonson is responsible for the line we all know so well: *"Drink to me only with thine eyes / And I will pledge with mine."* The allure of erotic behavior and a potent brew is legendary. This is the simple truth behind a love potion. The erotic brew of heady liquors, imbued with herbal preparations and deliciously scented fruits or flowers, is calculated to alter the state of awareness of the recipient — to relax the nervous, and to excite the bored. Mix someone a love cocktail and you'll be issuing an invitation to perceive, and be perceived, on a wonderfully heightened plateau of senses. ♣ These venerated potions are also chosen for situations that are not specifically romantic: how to create a mood of bliss among guests and relatives you want to work a little happy magic over. There are potions that take you into the bathroom and the bedroom to sprinkle love elixirs in your most precious places. The bath products are particularly important, because they ask you to think well of yourself — which is the most bewitching ingredient when you are seeking to find or improve a love relationship. ♣ In the pages ahead we include suggestions for the most appropriate vessels and "props" to accompany your potions: goblets, jugs and carafes, perfume phials, and even "poison rings" that set the mood and improve the potency of the blends. Some potions are summery, and some perfect for chilly weather. Some are alcoholic, and some not. All will invite the one you love to recapture an essence of romance and help lift your love relationship out of the commonplace. If you cannot create a significant impact with these precious potions, you must be working on the wrong person. ♣ Remember to pay attention to the aesthetics, and pick pretty flowers, herbs, and colors; all of these elements have an impact, and will increase the effectiveness of the spell. If you must make use of dried herbs or flowers — because the fresh plants are out of season or because you have no access to the fresh-grown version — you will still elicit a good response from these ingredients. See if you can add just a few fresh

petals from at least one of the herbs or flowers, just to add potency and visual appeal to the dried ones. ✿ DON'T FORGET, HOWEVER, THAT IT'S QUITE EASY TO GROW MANY HERBS AND SPECIAL LITTLE FLOWERS (LIKE PRIMROSES, LAVENDER, AND VIOLETS) IN A LARGE POT ON A WINDOWSILL OR A BALCONY. It is always uplifting to use some of your own things in magical recipes, and if you also grow them with love, they have added powers and charms. ✿ SO NOW IT'S TIME TO LEARN A NEW LANGUAGE OF BAR SKILLS AND CREATE SOME POWERFULLY POTENT MESSAGES. Create amazing opportunities to use the liquid treats—perhaps by sending forth delightful, handwritten invitations (with scented ink, of course) to a witchy afternoon tea party. Find wonderful china and have more than one set, so that your mood can dictate the pace. Perhaps you'll only want two cups and a pot. ✿ ALWAYS WORK YOUR MAGIC ON PEOPLE WHO ARE FREE TO ACCEPT YOUR LOVING INVITATIONS: DON'T POACH. Witches must be wise and good, as well as powerful. ✿ BLESSED BE.

Honoring the self ✿ WE BEGIN WITH A SHORT RITUAL, THOUGH, TO

MAKE YOU FEEL POWERFUL, SELF-AWARE, AND FRANKLY, BEWITCHING! Your magic will work better, and your charms have more voltage, if you begin with this very simple recipe for self-confidence. Don't leave it out. ✿ LET THIS RITUAL STAND AS A PRELUDE TO ALL YOUR MAGIC-WORKING AND POTION-MIXING. It is really simple to do, and you will feel a new sense of being in control of your own affairs. Any and all magic works best when you have a calm sense of belief in yourself.

You will need

a small photo of yourself; thin ribbons to embroider with; a small heart-shaped frame, preferably silver; small votive candles, pink or white; a sprig of rosemary; a glass of your favorite wine

❀ Work on a full, or nearly full, moon. ❀ Make a very simple altar at the hearth of your home, or in a quiet, private corner, and decorate it every few days with simple fresh flowers in colors you like. Then, on the evening of a full moon, trim your favorite photo of yourself—perhaps taken at a truly happy moment when you felt terrific—into a small heart shape. Using a wide-eyed darning needle, "embroider" the edges using very narrow ribbons—of a variety of colors, or predominantly of pinks, which represent love. You can just do a very simple whip stitch around the edge—or something more elaborate if you like. Make sure you "caress" yourself mentally—sing, chant sweet thoughts of happiness, and imagine sunshine-filled days and all your affairs of the heart being positive. Setting this visual scene is very important and will do more good to the image you project than you can possibly imagine. ❀ When you have completed your self-honoring talisman, put it in a little frame, ideally of silver to tap the rays of the moon, and place it on your altar. Light a little candle beside it each day of the lunar month, always seeing your sense of yourself growing. If you have had bad luck before, imagine the waning moon (for the first two weeks after full) cleansing away all the negativity. Then see the growing moon ushering in a time of romance and strong, magnetic personal appeal. From here on out, your luck in love will alter decidedly, and you will feel wonderfully aligned with the powers of the romantic moon. ❀ Now you're ready for a brew or two.

MAGIC COCKTAILS

We commence our education in blending brews with the intoxicating kind. Here, we carefully balance alcoholic beverages with a storehouse of herbs and flowers, chosen for their capacity to enhance the endorphin-releasing qualities in the potion—a combination of ingredients that give you a brilliant feel-good factor. The first few are very easy to make. But, if you're feeling ambitious and really inclined to master the witchery of potions, put your touch to the last couple, which require a little home-brewing of the alcohol itself: the results will be worth it. Make sure you choose an appropriate recipient, someone who is free to give you his or her unbridled affection.

Sweet violet wine ❀ THE ANCIENT GREEKS HAD A DEEP RESPECT FOR THE

VIOLET. A symbol of fertility, it was one of the most frequently used ingredients in love potions. Certainly, the properties of the flower make us feel healthy and happy, and also impart a very becoming glow to the skin. Violets also leave a wonderful aftertaste in the mouth, sweetening the breath invitingly. Try this blend with your lover—you'll enjoy the flavor as well as the effect.

YOU WILL NEED

4½ ounces fresh violets, or 1 teaspoon dried; 2½ cups sugar; 3 violet flowers per person, to decorate; 1 bottle very dry white wine

❀ TWO DAYS BEFORE THE POTION IS REQUIRED, PUT YOUR FRESH OR DRIED FLOWERS INTO 2 CUPS BOILING WATER, COVER THE PAN, AND LET COOL. Leave this mixture to steep for at least 12 hours. The day before the potion is required, strain the liquid into a heavy-bottomed saucepan, and add the sugar. Bring gently to a boil, and then simmer for about an hour at low heat until the mixture becomes syrupy. Cool, then pour into a bottle that you can stop with a cork. ❀ ON THE DAY YOU WISH TO SERVE YOUR POTION, DIP THE DECORATIVE VIOLETS BRIEFLY INTO THE CORDIAL, SHAKE OFF THE EXCESS LIQUID, AND DUST WITH A LITTLE SUGAR. Allow these to dry for 10 minutes. While you wait, put flute-shaped glasses into the freezer; when they are taken out they will become deliciously frosty. Now put 2 teaspoons of violet cordial into each glass, fill with the white wine, and strew the flowers on top. Serve right away, and wait for temperatures to rise.

Summer strawberries ❀ FROM A PURELY PHYSICAL POINT OF VIEW,

WILD STRAWBERRIES HAVE A VERY POSITIVE EFFECT ON THE DIGESTIVE SYSTEM AND ALSO FRESHEN THE MOUTH WONDERFULLY. Perhaps for this reason, a meal that is accompanied by strawberry potions is likely to evoke a frisky, get-together sort of inclination, rather than leaving you both feeling too heavy for passion. Strawberries are also high in iron and potassium, and may be just the thing to inject a little energy into your lover's fatigued spirits. If you think it is tiredness and the humdrum nature of life that is preventing you and your lover from being amorous, try this.

YOU WILL NEED

A good handful fresh strawberry leaves, or 1 tablespoon dried; 1 cup white wine; a good squeeze of lemon juice; 2 teaspoons sugar (optional for taste); 3½ ounces wild or alpine strawberries (or substitute cultivated); 1 bottle good-quality champagne

❀ FIRST MAKE A DECOCTION FROM THE LEAVES BY PLACING THEM IN 2 CUPS RAPIDLY BOILING WATER FOR ABOUT 10 MINUTES, UNTIL THE LIQUID REDUCES TO ABOUT HALF. Set aside to cool completely. Strain the liquid into a jug, and pour in the wine and lemon juice. Add in the sugar if desired. Steep this mixture for several hours in the refrigerator—from morning until evening would be excellent. Chill two glasses in the freezer for at least 30 minutes prior to serving. ❀ TO SERVE THE POTION, slice the strawberries in half (or into fine slices, if you're using the commercial variety), put them in the glasses, pour in the chilled mixture, then top the glass with the well-chilled champagne. Decorate the edge of the glass with just one strawberry, poised fetchingly over the lip. After a few sips, you should feel a little rush of returning strength and cheer.

Borage and bliss ✿ There is simply no other herb like borage.

This plant has long had a reputation for creating a lovely, gentle euphoria, and it is now understood that it does, indeed, stimulate adrenaline and combat depression. If you are lucky enough to be able to grow this beautiful, blue star-flower plant in a pot or in the garden, use it as a source to experiment with the flowers as additives to drinks and cooking. As a potion, this borage drink would be the best choice to encourage a relationship that is flagging, or to push an attraction on to the next stage. You will also find a mulled, winter variant with borage on page 40.

You will need
Juice of 1 lemon; 2 tablespoons honey; 2–3 borage leaves, finely chopped; a few borage flowers or 2 teaspoons borage tea; 2 cups white wine with a high alcohol content (about 13 percent)

✿ First make a homemade lemonade by adding the lemon juice and honey to 2 cups boiling water, dissolving well, and chilling in the refrigerator. To this chilled mixture, add the leaves and flowers (or tea), and chill for another hour. An hour before you require the potion, mix the borage lemonade with the strong wine in a carafe and leave to blend and steep in the refrigerator. Strain out the borage leaves, but replace the flowers, and serve in bluish glasses. ✿ The aesthetics and potency will be enhanced if you create some borage ice cubes to float in the glasses. Fill an ice-cube tray with water and put a flower in each compartment. Freeze. These will keep for some time after the borage flowers cease to bloom in late fall.

Alecost brew ❧ THIS IS BASED ON A DELICIOUS-SMELLING, TASTY HERB WHICH HAD BECOME UNFASHIONABLE, BUT IS MAKING A COMEBACK. If you want to order it from a retailer, the Latin name is *Balsamita major*, or sometimes *Tanacetum balsamita* (costmary). It is not hard to find if you go to a specialty store. The common name derives, as you might expect, from its ability to flavor ale or beer; it has a minty flavor which becomes more lemony when it is heated in food or drinks. Alecost has a very fortifying effect, bringing alertness when imbibed, which makes it the right choice if your beloved is always too tired for amorous adventures. The leaves are often added to potpourris to intensify the fragrance of the other herbs. Try it to intensify a relationship.

YOU WILL NEED
½ ounce dried alecost (costmary); 2 tablespoons vodka or kirsch; slices of lemon; a few sugared rose petals, to decorate; a little lemon juice

❧ INFUSE THE HERB IN 1 CUP FRESHLY BOILED WATER FOR TEN MINUTES, THEN STRAIN AND CHILL. Make the potion by pouring the vodka or kirsch into a whisky glass, topping with ice and lemon slices, and doubling the volume with the infused alecost (about ½ cup of the liquid). Decorate the glass with rose petals that have been dipped in lemon juice and then dusted with sugar. You will now have your beloved's fullest attention. ❧ ACCENTUATE THE "ALECOST EFFECT" BY ADDING SOME OF THE LEAVES TO YOUR FAVORITE POTPOURRI (PREFERABLY ONE THAT IS ROSE- OR CITRUS-BASED) AND PLACING THIS NEAR YOUR SITTING AREA. The smells will make both of you very alert.

Elderberry-flower laughter ✿ THIS UTTERLY SUMMERTIME

RECIPE WILL DEMAND A LITTLE MORE LABOR, AS YOU MAKE AN ELDERBERRY-FLOWER CHAMPAGNE OF YOUR OWN AS THE BASE. Of course, if you really can't be bothered, you can add commercial elderberry-flower cordial to a bottle of champagne and proceed from there, but it won't be quite the same. The magical content of the elderberry is long attested, (at one time, this tree was associated exclusively with witchcraft), which is why you should handle the flowers yourself, if possible. The flavor is wonderful, and it is believed that anyone drinking a potion of elderberry flowers in company with a potential lover is apt to feel a very powerful bond for many a long year. Try it and see.

YOU WILL NEED

10 very large, fully open elderberry flower "heads"; 8½ cups pure spring water; 1¼ cups sugar; 2 lemons, sliced; dash white wine vinegar; a few violet flowers or lilac florets, to decorate

✿ MAKE SURE THE ELDERBERRY FLOWER HEADS ARE CLEAN AND DRY. Bring the spring water to a boil in a jam-making pan (or cauldron), remove from the heat, and dissolve the sugar in the water, stirring constantly. Cover, and set the liquid aside to cool. Only when the liquid is cool should you add the elderberry flowers, stirring softly; then add the lemon slices and a dash of white wine vinegar. Cover again and leave somewhere cool to steep for three days. ✿ STRAIN THE CONTENTS THROUGH A MUSLIN BAG, THEN POUR THE LIQUOR INTO STERILIZED BOTTLES. You will need to cork them carefully, and it is advisable to wire the corks to prevent the mixture from blowing them off. Allow the bottles to stand for about a week, then chill well. Serve in chilled, frosty goblets, and put a scattering of violets or lilac florets on the top of the potion. The mixture is quite heady and will certainly intoxicate the senses. Do not drive afterward!

Love potion dessert ❧ THIS IS ANOTHER RECIPE THAT REQUIRES

LITTLE CAULDRON-STIRRING. It will work deliciously as a dessert if you are trying to encourage someone's feelings for you. The secret is to be completely relaxed and let the recipe do the hard work for you. Although it takes a little bit of time, it is a perfect option for the potion-maker who is city-bound and cannot get fresh herbs and flowers easily. If you're a supermarket shopper, this is your potion.

> YOU WILL NEED
>
> *1 pound ripe berries in season (such as raspberries, blueberries, or red and black currants);*
> *1 cup sugar; 1 bottle dessert wine (such as Muscatel, Beaume de Venise, or Sauternes); rose*
> *petals or other florets, to decorate*

❧ USE A MIXTURE OF DIFFERENT BERRIES TO GET THE MOST POTENT AND DELICIOUS EFFECT. Put the different berries in layers in sterilized jars, and sprinkle a layer of sugar across each layer of fruit as you go. Just before you reach the top of the jar, fill the rest with the dessert wine. Then cover, seal, and store the jars in a cool place. ❧ LET THE POTION DEVELOP FOR AT LEAST A WEEK BEFORE DIPPING INTO THE WICKEDLY WONDERFUL FLAVORS. Serve as a dessert with a good spoonful of thick plain yogurt and a light dusting of raw sugar. Sprinkle rose petals or other florets on top—once again, lilac is a beautiful and sense-intoxicating choice. This has a decided love potion effect.

SWEET CORDIALS

HERE WE LOOK AT WAYS TO MAKE THE SENSES HEADY WITHOUT INTOXICATION. If you're a teetotaler or too young to drink or are driving home afterward, these are the brews for you. None of them requires alcohol, and they are delicious without it. You could, however, add most of the mixtures straight to a glass of champagne or wine if you wished. Try to get your ingredients fresh: dried herbs and flowers do some of the job, but they never have quite as much impact as their fresher relations.

True love's brew ✿

ROSES WILL APPEAR AND REAPPEAR ON THESE PAGES, FOR ROSES ARE "GOOD FOR THE SKIN AND THE SOUL," AS THE SAYING GOES. They are the basis of more than 95 percent of all women's fragrances, and the petals have long been prized in medicine for cheering the spirits and soothing depression. *Rosa damascena*, in particular, is believed to be good for those who lack love, while *Rosa centifolia*, the French rose oil base, has a reputation as an aphrodisiac. So find a top-quality purveyor of these magical blooms and mix your potion.

YOU WILL NEED

Petals from 5-6 fresh flowers of Rosa centifolia *or* Rosa damascena, *or ¾ ounce dried petals; 3-4 tablespoons honey; sparkling mineral water; extra rose petals, to decorate*

✿ HEAT THE PETALS AND THE HONEY TOGETHER GENTLY AND SIMMER FOR ABOUT 10 MINUTES UNTIL THE HONEY IS COMPLETELY SCENTED WITH THE ROSE. Strain the mixture through a muslin bag, and cool. ✿ TO SERVE A ROMANTIC COCKTAIL TO ENTICE YOUR LOVE TO RELAX AND SEE YOU IN A GLOWING LIGHT WHILE GIVING YOU BOTH A SENSE OF WELL-BEING, add 1 tablespoon to a chilled glass, top with mineral water, and stir. Add cubes of ice and strew with a few petals. Divine!

The primrose tea party ✿ THIS IS A WONDERFUL BREW FOR

A NERVOUS FIRST ENCOUNTER OR A DATE AFTER AN ARGUMENT. Cowslips and primroses (generally used interchangeably) have a marvelous knack of settling the nerves and arresting a panic attack, and have been used in potions to make couples more relaxed. They are also a delight to the eye and taste absolutely heavenly. Try them in this tea.

YOU WILL NEED

1 ounce fresh (preferably) or dried cowslip/primrose flowers; juice of half a lemon; sugar to taste

✿ MAKE A POT OF TEA WITH THE FLOWERS AND ABOUT 3 CUPS BOILING WATER. Use a teapot with a proper infuser if possible, so that all of the properties of the flowers remain when the tea is strained from within the pot. ✿ JUST BEFORE POURING A CUP, SQUEEZE A LITTLE LEMON JUICE INTO THE POT WITH A SMALL AMOUNT OF SUGAR (probably less than 1 teaspoon, unless you have a very sweet tooth), and serve in pretty cups of sunshine colors to lift the spirits and calm anxieties. If you can reserve a fresh flower to float in the top, so much the better. Don't forget to place a vase of fresh-smelling herbs and flowers on the tea table, too.

Heartsease ♣ THIS USES THE BEAUTIFUL WILD PANSY (common name, heartsease;

Latin name, *Viola tricolor*) which—along with violet—was one of the most popular additives to the love potions of the ancient Greeks and Romans, as well as to those of their European descendants. The flower has also been called "kiss me in the buttery" and "love lies bleeding." Besides soothing the spirits, making a wonderful tonic for the heart and blood, and combating the exhaustion of an overlong day, this magical little flower will give a lovely glow to your complexion as you imbibe. An excellent choice for lovers who have become a little jaded.

YOU WILL NEED
Juice of 1 lemon; 2 tablespoons sugar; 2½ ounces wild pansy leaves and flowers—leaves chopped, flowers whole; sparkling mineral or elderberry-flower water, to serve; slice of lemon and 1-2 fresh flowers, to decorate

♣ MAKE A LEMONADE BY DISSOLVING THE LEMON AND SUGAR IN 2 CUPS BOILING WATER, STIRRING WELL. Set this mixture aside to cool, and meanwhile infuse the pansy leaves and flowers in the liquid. After at least an hour, bring the whole mixture to a boil again very quickly, allowing the boiling to continue for just 30 seconds. Remove from the heat, cool, and chill in the refrigerator. ♣ SERVE THIS POTION BY STRAINING IT INTO A TALL GLASS AND MIXING WITH EQUAL PARTS SPARKLING MINERAL OR ELDERBERRY-FLOWER WATER. Decorate with a slice of lemon and one or two fresh flowers.

A summer cup ✿ THIS THREE-HERB BLEND IS THE BEST POTION TO USE IF

YOU'RE TRYING TO CHEER UP A WHOLE GATHERING OF PEOPLE. Less specific to love, and more to an overall feeling of happiness, mix this little cocktail if you're hosting a family get-together and want to keep the tensions under control. Of course, it's also excellent for cheering up your partner if he or she is a bit low or under too much pressure due to work or health.

YOU WILL NEED

½ ounce fresh marjoram or oregano leaves or 1 teaspoon dried; ½ ounce fresh lemon balm leaves or 1 teaspoon dried; 5 flowers of Rosa gallica *or* Rosa damascena*; 2 tablespoons sugar; juice of 1 lemon, plus some lemon slices; 1 (resealable) bottle sparkling mineral or soda water*

✿ STEEP ALL THE INGREDIENTS, EXCEPT THE SPARKLING WATER, TOGETHER IN A SMALL PAN FOR ABOUT ONE HOUR, THEN ADD JUST ONE TABLESPOON OF WATER TO THE PAN AND HEAT GENTLY FOR A FEW MINUTES. Cool; then, using a funnel, pour all the ingredients, without straining, into the bottle of sparkling water. Carefully turn the bottle on end a few times, then place it in the refrigerator and chill thoroughly. Serve through a tea strainer into a glass with crushed ice, and decorate with a few slices of lemon. ✿ IF YOUR GATHERING INCLUDES GUESTS WHO HAVE NO OBJECTION TO ALCOHOL, ADD A DASH OF VODKA TO THE GLASS AS WELL: IT'S DELICIOUS!

Pink drink

❀ THIS IS REGARDED AS A POTENT FLOWER POTION, because carnations (which we call "pinks" when talking about the old-fashioned variety with the strong perfume) were used to spice up wines and foods, and were also a symbol of passionate love to the Romans—as they still are to modern Italians. They have a wonderful clove-like taste, but you must use the real thing—called clove pink or clove carnation. Sipping this with someone you like quite well could move the relationship onto a higher plateau.

YOU WILL NEED

1 cinnamon stick; petals from about 6 clove carnations (about 3½ ounces fresh flowers); a pinch ground ginger; ½ cup firmly packed brown sugar; 2 cups spring water; a few drops of glycerine; sparkling mineral water, to serve

❀ PUT THE FIRST FIVE INGREDIENTS IN A SAUCEPAN AND BRING VERY SLOWLY TO A BOIL, STIRRING CONTINUOUSLY. Reduce the heat and simmer for about 10 minutes; when the syrup begins to thicken, remove from the heat and cool. Add a few drops of glycerine and the mixture will become pinker.

❀ MAKE UP YOUR POTION BY STRAINING ABOUT 2 TABLESPOONS OF THIS LIQUID INTO A GLASS AND TOPPING OFF WITH SPARKLING MINERAL WATER. If you're not being a teetotaler, it is also delicious added to champagne, and will turn it a gentle rose color.

Moroccan mint tea ❀ THIS IS A LOVELY, SILENT LOVE POTION. It does

not announce its intentions loudly, but quietly concludes a meal, leaving lovely fresh mouths longing to entangle and adding a touch of energy to carry you both on for a while. Choose this if you want to sneak up on your loved one and leave him or her with a lingering desire for you.

YOU WILL NEED

4 sprigs fresh mint (preferably powerful Moroccan spearmint); 1 tablespoon dried china or jasmine tea leaves; 2 cups boiling water; 1 teaspoon sugar; crushed ice

❀ CRUSH THE MINT INTO A TEAPOT AND ADD THE TEA LEAVES AND BOILING WATER. Allow the tea to infuse for about 10 minutes, then stir in the sugar. Cool. Serve the tea strained onto crushed ice in a Moroccan tea glass, decorated with just one or two mint leaves; or if it is a cold night, simply serve warmed in the tea glasses. The tea will relax you while it promotes sweet breath and a gentle sense of desire. A friend of mine—fast becoming a love diva—places a pot of this tea beside her bed (with two cups) so that she and her lover can wake up each morning in mint condition. She says nothing invites a morning kiss better than this.

MULLED MAGIC

THESE DELICIOUSLY SCENTED BREWS ARE FOR CHILLY DAYS, when cuddling up and sipping warm drinks by the fire with someone gorgeous is one of the best respites from the cold weather. Don't wait for the winter festivities to try them out: blend and brew from the end of the fall onward.

Blackberry brew ❧ BLACKBERRY IS A FAVORED CHOICE FOR TREATING

GENERAL FATIGUE, BUT ALSO STIRS THE SPIRITS SENSUALLY. It has a very "witchy" connection, being a staple ingredient in potions in Britain. This brew is, incidentally, wonderful for Christmas, but it will warm a cool heart as well. Blueberries could be used if blackberries are unavailable.

YOU WILL NEED
2¼ pounds blackberries; 2½ cups sugar; 1 ounce whole cloves; 1 cinnamon stick; ½ nutmeg (unground); 1 cup brandy; shreds of cinnamon bark, to serve

❧ CAREFULLY HULL THE BLACKBERRIES, THEN PLACE THEM IN A FOOD PROCESSOR WITH 2 OR 3 TABLESPOONS OF THE SUGAR AND BLEND TO A PULPY PURÉE. Put the purée in a heavy-bottomed saucepan with the remaining sugar and the spices, cover, and bring gently to a boil. At the first real bubble reduce to a simmer, and cook for about 20 minutes. Remove from the heat and allow to cool, then add the brandy and stir until well combined. Strain the liquid through a muslin bag into bottles (it will make about 4 cups), and cork. ❧ ALLOW THE BREW TO DEVELOP FOR ABOUT A WEEK, THEN WARM JUST A LITTLE AT A TIME (ONLY AS MUCH AS YOU WISH TO SERVE) OVER LOW HEAT IN A SAUCEPAN. Serve in shot glasses with a few shreds of cinnamon bark. It should not be steaming hot, but very warming.

Mulled raspberry vodka ❧ RASPBERRY HAS POWERS OF RESCUE:

it is a favorite choice for postnatal women and an excellent all-around winter pick-me-up. Here, it lends its delicious flavor to vodka, and the double effect is one of relaxed well-being. Either use the fruit from the last fall crop, or buy some commercially grown.

> YOU WILL NEED
>
> *9 ounces (about 2¼ cups) fresh raspberries, plus a few to decorate; 2 tablespoons honey;*
> *a squeeze of lemon juice; juice of 1 orange; vodka, to serve*

❧ PROCESS THE RASPBERRIES, HONEY, AND JUICES IN A BLENDER UNTIL VERY LIQUID AND THICK. Press through a strainer, add a little water, and bottle in the refrigerator for a day (it will make about 2 cups). ❧ JUST BEFORE YOU SERVE IT ON THE FOLLOWING DAY/EVENING, warm the purée very gently in a pan, and then add 1 or 2 teaspoons to a small shot of vodka, with a raspberry floating on the top (the cocktail should be body temperature). Take it carefully, for it has a powerful tendency to intoxicate.

Witches' wassail ✿ THIS IS MOST EFFICACIOUS FOR CREATING A LITTLE

GENTLE REVELRY. Borage, which we have already encountered on page 16, is the principal ingredient, and the brew makes a wonderful Yule wassail for getting a whole company of friends into a euphoric state. It will, however, work wonders as well with a solitary admirer.

YOU WILL NEED

Leaves and about a dozen flowers of borage; 1¾ ounces cubed pieces of toasted whole-wheat bread; ½ cup raw sugar; 3 sugar cubes, saturated with Grand Marnier or Cointreau; ½ nutmeg (unground); 1 cinnamon stick; a pinch each of ground ginger and cloves; 1 tablespoon orange-flower water; a little orange peel; 4 cups stout or brown ale, depending on your taste; 4 cups flower wine (elderberry-flower or bilberry, or mead if available)

✿ MIX ALL THE INGREDIENTS TOGETHER IN A WASSAIL BOWL (A LARGE PUNCH BOWL IS A MODERN EQUIVALENT). Start with the borage leaves, finely diced, and the toast, then add the sugar, the sugar cubes, the spices, the orange-flower water, and the orange peel. Warm the stout and the wine in a large saucepan (do not boil) and add them to the wassail bowl, a little at a time, stirring well between additions, until the whole mixture is well blended. Finally, scatter the borage flowers over the brew, and allow to stand for about 10 minutes until you are ready to serve. It is nice if you can keep it over a low burner, so try to find an appropriate vessel. ✿ BORAGE FLOWERS WELL INTO THE FALL, but if you cannot get borage flowers in the winter, and have none put by from summer days, use some borage tea from a good specialty store and choose another flower for strewing over the bowl at the end. Rose petals or orange peel also work very well for this.

Wild oats ✿ THE EXPRESSION "TO SOW YOUR OATS" MIGHT ALMOST BE BASED ON THE PROPERTY OF OATS TO FORTIFY THE BODY AND RELEASE THE SOUL FROM SADNESS. Saffron, of course, is also an aphrodisiac, so use this in small quantities. So effective can this potion be, that it might be best to warn: HANDLE WITH CARE!

YOU WILL NEED

1 bottle dry white wine; 3 tablespoons dried oats; 1 tablespoon rolled oats; a pinch of saffron (the real thing, please!); a pinch of cinnamon; 1 teaspoon honey; a few gardenia flower petals

✿ HEAT THE WINE VERY GENTLY AND ADD IN ALL THE OTHER INGREDIENTS, STIRRING AS YOU GO. Simmer at very low heat for about 10 minutes, then strain through a tea strainer into a two-handled cup, Irish coffee glasses, or punch glasses. Serve just before bed!

This would be extra-effective if you sprayed the bed linen lightly with some cinnamon and gardenia perfume. It will carry the mood deliciously.

41

Plum for love THIS IS ONE OF THE MOST POWERFUL AND POTENT HERBAL TONICS. IT can be used all year round, but is particularly uplifting in the colder months. It centers on plum and rosemary, which treat fatigue and depression; but, if you can enlist the extra herbal tonic power of the damiana—which acts on the male hormonal system while remedying female anxiety and lack of sexual appetite—it will really add a special element to this absolutely wonderful and true love potion.

YOU WILL NEED

Just over 1 pound red or purple plums, pitted and sliced; ¾ cup and 2 tablespoons sugar; 1 cup spring water; 3 good sprigs rosemary; ⅓ ounce citric acid; ½ ounce powdered damiana, if available; red or white wine, or champagne, to serve

SIMMER THE PLUMS, SUGAR, WATER, AND ROSEMARY IN A LARGE SAUCEPAN FOR ABOUT 15–20 MINUTES, UNTIL SOFT AND FRAGRANT. When cool, process the mixture in a blender, then strain into a jug and stir in the citric acid. Bottle this if you are going to keep it for a few weeks, or it will last in a jug in the refrigerator, covered with plastic wrap, for a few days. BEFORE SERVING, SPRINKLE IN THE DAMIANA (IF USING) AND STIR WELL. Then pour into a glass cordial-style and top with red or white wine (slightly warmed if you like), or even champagne. The recipe will make about 2 cups of cordial, so will last you several days.

Blood red roses ✿ ONE OF MY PERSONAL FAVORITES, THIS POTION IS
DELICIOUS, WARMING, AND SUBTLE, BUT WILL INDUCE GOOD HUMOR FOR YOU AND YOUR
LOVED ONE. It is also nice to serve to a gathering of friends if they all need a little help with sagging spirits.

YOU WILL NEED

*1 tablespoon fresh rosemary flowers; 3 tablespoons fresh red rose petals (with a strong scent);
3 or 4 violet leaves, chopped well; 1 bottle good-quality red wine*

✿ ALLOW ALL OF THE INGREDIENTS TO STEEP IN THE RED WINE FOR A FEW HOURS IN A WARM
PLACE. Before pouring the brew, warm goblets by filling them with hot water and then emptying them
out. Strain the potion into the goblets and serve. If you prefer, you can decant the wine into a dramatic
vessel, after first straining out the greenery!

These ingredients are obviously easiest to find in the summer, yet the brew suits colder, perhaps autumnal days. The solution is to freeze the flowers and violet leaves in a little freezer bag, where they can remain happily for a couple of months, extending your sense of summer. But do try to get some fresh red roses at least, for garnish.

BODY ELIXIRS

OUR BRAINS REGISTER SMELL IN A VERY SPECIFIC PLACE, IN THE ZONE NEXT TO THAT WHICH PRODUCES THE HORMONES AFFECTING STRESS AND ANXIETY. Because of this proximity, perfumes trigger a change in our breathing, and slow us down gently. In this chapter and the next, we look at different potions based on scent, first concentrating on bathing and massage.

START WITH A PROPER RITUAL FOR THE BATH, TO GET READY FOR LOVE; then, progress to the art of massage. Using scent, you can send subtle messages to your beloved without having to use words.

Basic body language ✿ MASSAGE IS THE MOST EFFECTIVE FOREPLAY,

since touch releases endorphins (the feel-good chemicals), and coupled with these olfactory delights, will send your lucky recipient into the realms of bliss. Happily, your nose gets its fair share of pleasure, even if it is not your body being pampered. The oils are an expensive investment perhaps, but will go far and last long.

YOU WILL NEED

3-4 tablespoons almond, or almond and avocado, oil; 5 drops each rose otto (attar)
and jasmine essential oils; 3 drops neroli essential oil; 2 drops sandalwood essential oil

✿ MAKE THIS BLEND AT LEAST ONE NIGHT BEFORE, TO ALLOW THE ESSENTIAL OILS TIME TO STEEP IN THE CARRIER OIL. However, it is also wise to use up the mixture within a week, for the essential oils lose their height of potency after this period unless they are kept cool in their dark bottles. Jasmine invites mystery and stirs the hormones toward sensuality, while rose works on areas of deep memory—promoting a powerful storehouse of future recollections of this sensual moment.

✿ MAKE YOUR MASSAGE STROKES LONG AND UNHURRIED, combining a basic long stroke with very gentle kneading for muscle spasms and gently playful pinches for love. This potion works absolute wonders, so take pleasure in your stroking and do not hurry its application.

Acceleration tonic ❀

IF YOU THINK IT HAS BEEN TAKING TOO LONG FOR YOUR LOVE AFFAIR TO MOVE ONTO A MORE POWERFULLY SENSUAL PLANE, TRY THIS MASSAGE OIL RATHER THAN THE PREVIOUS, MORE SUBTLE VERSION. This is less about romance and more about basic instinct.

YOU WILL NEED

FOR THE FEMALE PARTNER: *3-4 tablespoons almond or olive oil; 4 drops each jasmine and sweet myrtle oils; 3 drops cinnamon oil; 3 drops vanilla essence; 2 drops patchouli oil; pink ribbon*

FOR THE MALE PARTNER: *3-4 tablespoons jojoba oil; 3 drops each frankincense, lavender, black pepper, and coriander oils; blue ribbon*

❀ MIX UP EACH POTION, BLENDING THE OILS THE PREVIOUS DAY AND ALLOWING THEM TO STEEP IN PRETTY LITTLE BOTTLES. Tie a pink ribbon around the female bottle and a blue around the male. Make sure you bring champagne to the massage room, and that both of you are partaking. The smells are really intoxicating, and the feel of the oils on the body will be divine. ❀ THE OIL IS DESIGNED TO BE APPLIED ANYWHERE!

The kiss ❧ THE NEED FOR A DELICIOUSLY INVITING MOUTH CANNOT BE OVERSTATED—

it can turn a partner on faster than any other behavioral language. This mouthwash is designed to be used fresh and will beat a commercial potion hands down. Pop it into a plant mister or a perfume atomizer, and utilize its powers after a meal. If the weather is warm, keep it in the refrigerator and quietly apply when you put the last of the cheeses or dessert away.

YOU WILL NEED

½ cup spring water; 6 whole cloves; 1 tablespoon chopped parsley; the zest of 1 orange; 2 tablespoons orange-flower water; 2 drops orange essential oil; 1 teaspoon cumin seeds

❧ PUT ALL THE OTHER INGREDIENTS IN THE SPRING WATER AND BRING GENTLY TO A BOIL. The mixture should be cooled, strained, and then stored in a lidded jar in the refrigerator. Shake before each usage, and use about 1 tablespoonful at a time, rinsing completely. This potion will last up to a week in the refrigerator.

Wake-him-up bath potion ✤ You need to invigorate

YOUR SENSES AND THOSE OF YOUR PARTNER IF TIREDNESS OR COMPLACENCE ARE YOUR BIGGEST ENEMIES TO ROMANCE. This makes a powerfully energizing bath or shower gel, and will invite a more enthusiastic approach to the hours ahead. You need not wait for daybreak, though. A quick pick-up after the dash home from work is perfect.

> You will need
>
> *4 teaspoons baby shampoo; 2 teaspoons almond or baby oil; 2 drops bergamot essential oil;*
> *2 drops rosemary essential oil (excites the male libido); 2 drops lemon or orange essential oil;*
> *1 teaspoon witch hazel solution (to calm the skin)*

✤ SHAKE ALL THE INGREDIENTS TOGETHER IN A BOTTLE, THEN WET YOUR SKIN IN THE SHOWER THOROUGHLY BEFORE APPLYING THIS BREEZY MIXTURE TO THE BODY WITH A SPONGE OR WASH-CLOTH. If you are using it in the bath, pour some under the rushing water at the beginning of drawing the bath, and add a little also in the last moment to get the prime inhalation effect from the oils. ✤ THIS MAKES ENOUGH POTION FOR TWO BATHS OR SHOWERS; FOR BEST EFFECT, SHARE THE BOTTLE OR THE BATH WITH THAT IMPORTANT SOMEONE! Don't forget the importance of presentation, and choose the best decanters you can find. Handwrite your labels in pretty writing, and tie a sprig of fresh rosemary at the collar of the bottle with a wake-up ribbon in yellow, orange, or green.

Enchanted waters bath soak ✿ IF YOUR AIM IS TO MAKE

A FLORAL INVITATION TO BE HUGGED AND PETTED IN A TRULY ROMANTIC WAY, and you need to calm him down and make him relaxed rather than pep him up, use this potion instead of the previous one. Remember how famously milk was used by a certain Cleopatra to charm her high-powered men.

YOU WILL NEED

A scant 2 tablespoons whole milk; 4 teaspoons scentless (or mildly rose-scented) liquid hand and body soap; 4 drops rose essential oil; 4 drops lavender essential oil; 2 tablespoons rosewater; 1 tablespoon fresh rose petals

✿ SHAKE THE INGREDIENTS TOGETHER IN A SMALL BOTTLE, AND ALLOW TO STEEP FOR A FEW MINUTES. Pour the contents into the bath water and soak. For best results, tie a pink ribbon around your forehead as you bathe, as this will stimulate thoughts of gentle love. Share your bath, if possible, and don't forget the extra romantic power of a few fresh rose petals or buds scattered on the bath water. It's like love in a field of wild roses.

The hair bath ❧ THIS CELEBRATES THE DAYS WHEN FRAGRANT TRESSES WERE MORE UNUSUAL THAN THEY HAVE BECOME AS A RESULT OF DESIGNER SHAMPOOS. However, there is a special magic woven into these ingredients, and this is the base of a wonderful love spell.

YOU WILL NEED

1 tablespoon ground orrisroot; 1 tablespoon chopped fresh parsley; 1 tablespoon lavender buds; 3-4 tablespoons spring water; 4 drops lavender essential oil

❧ BLEND THE INGREDIENTS TOGETHER IN A BOTTLE AND ALLOW TO STEEP OVERNIGHT, THEN STRAIN THROUGH MUSLIN. Shampoo and lightly condition your hair as normal, then apply the elixir generously. Do not rinse. Think a spell of enchantment as you work, and watch as you bewitch your lover! **You do not need long tresses for this wondrous witchery. Just behave with full awareness that you have sassy hair! After using this potion, it should be extra shiny and soft to touch, too.**

FRAGRANT RAIN

Here we are concerned with making perfume—for ourselves and for our living space. Fragrance is a potent language of the natural world: from flowers, it is a call to be pollinated, ensuring futurity through unmitigated attraction. We borrow from their language to create a new one for ourselves—also, essentially, a call to be pollinated.

It is important to produce a blend of scents that work in unity together, and to formulate the right strength for the job you want to do. If you're young and sassy, create one of the "splash" blends, as this invites closeness because it's not overpowering, yet very friendly. If you're older and your scent needs to linger into the night, choose a more potent blend (15 percent essential oil, 85 percent carrier oil). Remember, though, that the art of seduction is always in under-, rather than *over*-, application.

Elixir of youth ✿ This is a perfect potion for the young — in years

or at heart! It will revive your spirits on a hot or too long day, because the scent is light and the combination of geranium and rose eases an overloaded mind. Spritz it onto your body after a shower, and then splash a little over your clothes, too.

You will need

3 teaspoons spring water; 3 teaspoons ethyl alcohol (from a drugstore, pharmacy or online source—see page 88); 5 drops rose oil; 5 drops bergamot oil; 5 drops rose geranium oil; 1 drop ginger oil

✿ Blend the ingredients in a small perfume bottle, preferably an atomizer if you have one. It will need shaking each time, and makes about 2 tablespoons. This is the ideal brew to entice the opposite sex without going overboard. It also promotes well-being in the wearer. Sprinkle or spray it lightly onto your sheets and in the curtains to spread the ambience around your dwelling place or office. **I shared this potion years ago with my Sydney neighbor, Zoë, who keeps some in her car to freshen it up, too. She works a special magic over everyone who travels with her.**

Cream potion ✿ MAKING THIS DELICIOUS CREAM HAS A DUAL PURPOSE, AS

YOU CAN PUT IT ON ANYWHERE FOR THE PLEASURE OF ITS SCENT AND ENRICH YOUR SKIN WHILE

YOU'RE AT IT. In the recipe on page 69, we take this process a step further, and make solid scent.

YOU WILL NEED

5 ¼ ounces emulsifying ointment (available from a pharmacy or online source—see page 88);
5 tablespoons glycerine; 2 teaspoons each of three floral essential oils of your choice (make rose
one of them); ⅓ ounce ground orrisroot

✿ ORRISROOT IS WONDERFUL FOR THE SKIN. It imparts a delicious fragrance and prolongs the "life"
of the other scents as well. Rose oil is likewise nourishing for the skin; your other two choices should be
tested to see if they blend harmoniously. ✿ MELT THE OINTMENT AND GLYCERINE VERY GENTLY IN
A BOWL OVER A PAN OF BOILING WATER (OR IN A DOUBLE BOILER), THEN ADD IN THE OILS AND
ORRISROOT AND CONTINUE TO HEAT FOR ABOUT 15 MINUTES. Strain through muslin and cool a little
before putting into jars using a broad palette knife: place the cream around the edges first, then fill up the
center. ✿ THIS CREAM WILL LAST FOR A FEW MONTHS IF STORED IN A DARK GLASS JAR AND KEPT
COOL. Remember to add a pretty label.

Intimacy ❀ HERE WE TURN UP THE VOLUME: this is the choice if you want to be absolutely sure you will not be ignored—by a stranger, a complacent lover, or a tired husband. It is only fair to add that you should be sure you wear this for someone who is entirely free to be enticed by you. It is out of keeping with white magic to use this as a "marriage breaker." Be careful!

YOU WILL NEED

4 teaspoons ethyl alcohol; 1 teaspoon spring water; 10 drops tuberose oil; 10 drops rose oil; 6 drops bergamot oil; 6 drops jasmine oil; 4 drops patchouli oil; 4 drops oakmoss oil; pure pheremone

❀ BLEND ALL THE INGREDIENTS CAREFULLY, EXCEPT THE PHEREMONE, AND PUT INTO A DARK, SMALL PHIAL FOR AT LEAST THREE WEEKS TO MATURE. When you are ready to use it, just dab it onto the wrists and dab one drop of pheremone under the nose. You will exude a potent self-confidence and allure, as well as a feeling of wonderful control.

Pheremone is available from good essential oil retailers (see page 88), and though expensive, is a long-term investment that will greatly increase the wearer's sense of well-being— thus making him or her more magnetic to others!

Potent pourri for marriage ❀ MIX THIS RECIPE FOR A

POTPOURRI IF YOU WANT TO PUT GENTLE VIBRATIONS TOWARD MARRIAGE INTO THE AIR, OR TO CONTINUE THE APHRODISIAC ELEMENT AFTER A HONEYMOON. Place it in the bedroom, and stir each day with your ring finger.

YOU WILL NEED
1 cup each fresh scented rose petals (pink or dark red), tiny roses, rosebuds, honeysuckle or jasmine flowers, lavender buds, and dried verbena; 2 tablespoons ground orrisroot; 2 drops each rose, jasmine, and lavender essential oils

❀ IN A PRETTY BOWL, BLEND ALL THE DRY INGREDIENTS TOGETHER, THEN THE OILS, AND STIR WELL. Cover for a few days with dark plastic to allow the scents to develop, but give the bowl an hour of fresh air each day to avoid the potpourri turning moldy. This mixture will now keep for months. The potency of its fragrance can be replenished by adding refresher doses of oils when required.

Fall-in-love fragrant potpourri ❀ THIS IS THE BEST

CHOICE FOR SIMPLY SCENTING THE AIR WITH NOTES OF LOVE. If you want to attract love to a new abode or even in your office, this is a subtle but reliable potpourri mixture. Plunder friends' gardens to get the fresh flowers you need.

> YOU WILL NEED
> *1 cup each fresh violets, sweet peas (mauve and pink for attracting love), scented clove carnations (pinks), sweet woodruff or meadowsweet, and peonies; 1 tablespoon ground orrisroot; 2 drops each violet, carnation, sweet pea, and peony essential or perfume oils*

❀ REMOVE THE PETALS OF THE LARGER FLOWERS AND KEEP SEVERAL WHOLE, SMALLER FLOWERS. Combine all the ingredients in a tightly lidded jar, adding the oils last. Store for four to six weeks in a dry, dark place, shaking the jar occasionally to blend the mixture. ❀ DECANT INTO AN APPROPRIATE VESSEL AND PLACE IN THE HEARTH, ON THE ALTAR OF YOUR HOME, OR RIGHT ON YOUR DESK AT WORK. Bliss for noses and spirits.

Solid scent ✿ THIS IS A WITCHY POTION FOR A FEMME FATALE. It is very evocative
and will give you a feeling of magical control at your fingertips as you stroke it on. Unlike the cream in the
recipe on page 63, which is absorbed into the skin, this balm forms a separate layer and will hold the scent
well. The best receptacle for it on a daily basis would be a small locket that you could wear around your
neck. Be sure to find your aromatic trademark by experimenting with several oils for the right balance.

YOU WILL NEED
½ ounce white beeswax; ½ ounce anhydrous lanolin; 60 ml (2 fluid ounces, about ¼ cup)
essential oils of your choice (try these groups: bergamot, lemon, neroli, orange; sandalwood, rose,
bergamot, jasmine; ylang ylang, clove, vanilla, tuberose; frankincense, petitgrain, bergamot,
ginger; rose, myrtle, sandalwood, oakmoss; neroli, lavender, vetiver)

✿ THIS WILL BE A COSTLY FIRST BREW, BUT WILL LAST WELL IF STORED IN A DARK GLASS JAR
AND KEPT COOL. Heat the beeswax and lanolin in a double boiler (or in a bowl over a pan of boiling
water), taking care to do this slowly and gently. While it is still warm, pour in your blend of oils (totaling
60 ml: most essential oils are available in 10 or 15 ml bottles), and stir well until properly combined. While
the mixture is still warm and molten, pour into clean, dark glass jars and label. ✿ WHEN YOU WANT TO
TAKE A LITTLE AND PUT IT INTO A LOCKET OR PERFUME RING, USE A WARM KNIFE TO REMOVE IT.
Be aware when and where you wear it—your body temperature can make the unguent too soft.

POTIONS TO GO

IN OUR FINAL CHAPTER WE MIX UP SOME INTERESTING ADDITIVES FOR MAKING A POTION ON THE HOP—WHEN YOU SIMPLY CAN'T PACK THE SAUCEPAN OR THE FOOD PROCESSOR. These simple tonics, powders, and cordials are easy to pack in a travel pouch, as it were, and will help you bring a more exciting element to a romantic weekend or even just an important day at the office. Here is an excuse for some wonderful props: pretty glass perfume phials with good stoppers will come into their own and can be filled with fascinating, sparkling diamond drops, while tiny lockets, lidded rings, and little blush or powder compacts can take on a whole new lease of life as the accessories of the femme fatale. Take a little shopping spree to find some items that inspire you.

The weekend pillow ✿ Two simple items you can mix up to

CREATE INSTANT ROMANTIC AMBIENCE AND SENSUALITY, when you are heading off for a weekend of (hopefully) love and passion.

YOU WILL NEED

FOR THE PILLOW POUCHES: *cotton cosmetic pads; blotting paper; a few drops each of rose, lavender, and neroli essential oils; muslin; ribbon*

FOR THE ROOM SPRAY: *3 drops each lavender, grapefruit, and lime essential oils; 2 tablespoons spring water*

✿ CUT THE COSMETIC PADS INTO LOVELY SHAPES—MOONS, STARS, HEARTS—AND DO THE SAME WITH THE BLOTTING PAPER. Make a blend of the oils in a small droppered bottle, and put a few drops onto the cotton and paper shapes, allowing them to dry for a few hours in a lidded box. Then put the scented shapes into a pouch made of muslin, and tie with a ribbon. Make two of these (you might prefer to spray your favorite perfume onto the shapes) and put one each inside your pillowcase and that of your love when you're away in a hotel or at a friend's house. Instant bewitchment! ✿ FOR THE SPRAY, shake the ingredients in a tiny perfume atomizer, then use it around the bathroom and sleeping area to neutralize smells of the previous occupant, add antiseptic reassurance, and create a more familiar and comfortable feel. Your love will soon be very relaxed and purring.

Violet dusting powder ♣ THIS EXTENDS THE MOOD OF SENSUAL

BATHING ON INTO THE NIGHT. We often forget the sheer sensuous thrill of our body, dusted with translucent powder, which thus becomes even more silky to the touch than it is with body lotion. Try this and you're sure to be a convert. Moreover, the scent of you is certain to linger in your love's imagination. You might use this in conjunction with the bath pouch (see page 76).

YOU WILL NEED

1 tablespoon cornstarch or arrowroot powder; 1 teaspoon ground orrisroot; a few fresh violets or other flower (one type of flower only)

♣ PLACE ALL THE INGREDIENTS IN A SMALL, TIGHTLY-LIDDED CARDBOARD BOX FOR A FEW DAYS UNTIL THE SMELLS BLEND TOGETHER: then pack them carefully into a small powder compact with a little puff. Dust your upper torso after bathing, and sprinkle the scent into lingerie and even the sheets. This powder is also easy to apply at the office between hectic moments to keep you cool and enticing, and is an absolute essential for a short break in a sunny climate. It looks divine in a beautiful glass dish with a few fresh violets added every few days.

Fragrant bath essence ✿ Many weekends away are enhanced

by nice bath products in the rooms; still, leave nothing to chance. This wonderful bath pouch easily slips into a carryall, will create a visual as well as scented high for you and your beloved, and should lead quickly to romance.

You will need
12-inch square of muslin; sprigs of fresh rosemary, lavender, pine, and lemon balm; a few drops each rosemary, lavender, pine, and lemon balm essential oils; pretty ribbon

✿ Make up a muslin bag for the bath with the fresh ingredients: rosemary is important for male sensual awareness and lemon balm for female. Add a few drops of the oils to intensify the smell, and tie the bag securely with a pretty ribbon (pink for love, red or shocking pink for passion, yellow for a pick-me-up). Position the bag underneath the faucet, where the water flows out into the bath, tying the ribbon around the taps to hold it. Prepare this before you go off for a walk, and return to a shared bath before dinner . . . but plan on eating late!

Poudre d'amour ❀ In days gone by, many an enchantress had a

HINGED RING IN WHICH SHE CARRIED POTENT POWDERS OR EVEN POISON. This sensual powder is a worthy and positive successor to the substances of that tradition. See if you can find an antique hinged ring to carry it in, and from which you can subtly dispense a few grains. This exotic powder is ideal for bestowing a serious pick-me-up which tends to playful, erotic friskiness as well. Dish this out to your beloved if passion is simply not on the menu any more. You can take it with you anywhere.

You will need

1 capsule of powdered ginseng; a pinch of powdered damiana (Turnera diffusa)*; 2 or 3 strands of saffron; a tiny pinch of ground coriander*

❀ Combine these four tonic, aphrodisiac herbs carefully, and put them into a dry, stable receptacle. Add them discreetly to a glass of ale or dry fermented cider, and they will soon perk up the imbiber. If you like, scatter a few rosemary or borage flowers in the glass, too, for aesthetic reasons as well as tonic effect. **This is a true brew for a femme fatale! See how adventurous you can be in finding ways to utilize its passsionate properties. It even adds a buzz to mineral water: use sparkling rather than still, since the bubbles work faster in the bloodstream.**

Moroccan magic elixir ❧

WE BORROW SOME OF THE INGREDIENTS OF THE WARMING AND APHRODISIAC RAS EL HANOUT FROM MOROCCO—OMITTING THE TREACHEROUS SPANISH FLY. If you are cooking for your beloved away from home, try adding this to a lamb stew or a chicken couscous dish. It can also be used in a hot wine. Just carry it with you in a tiny jar: you don't need to use too much.

YOU WILL NEED

A few strands of saffron; ½ teaspoon cumin seeds; pinch ground ginger; handful tiny rose buds

❧ WARM ALL THE INGREDIENTS TOGETHER VERY LIGHTLY IN A DRY PAN, OR IN THE OVEN, FOR JUST A FEW MOMENTS. Add them to your cooking or, for variation, try steeping them in some warmed red or white wine. Strain the mixture before decanting into a wine jug, and return just a few of the rose buds for decoration. A steamy invitation to a loving evening.

The "hip" flask

REINVENT THE APPEAL OF A HIP FLASK WITH THIS EXCELLENT RECIPE OF CHEERINESS FOR LOVERS. Perhaps if you are going cycling or walking together, or are just off for a warm weekend of romance, this will get you both in the mood.

YOU WILL NEED

1 teaspoon poppy seeds; 2 teaspoons dried jasmine flowers or a handful of fresh jasmine flowers; 2 bay leaves, crumbled; 5 tablespoons brandy

STEEP ALL THE INGREDIENTS IN A WARMED SAUCEPAN (BUT NOT DIRECTLY ON THE HEAT), IN A WARM PLACE, FOR AT LEAST AN HOUR: above the stove, or near some heating, would be ideal. Strain, then decant the liquid into a suitable hip flask. Sip with your beloved at regular intervals over a chilly weekend. Divine!

The perfume garden ❀ THIS APPENDIX IS DESIGNED TO HELP YOU

MAKE CHOICES FOR BLENDING YOUR OWN SCENT. The oils are grouped in families that blend well together, and you can play around to see which ones make up your preferred choice. By understanding the families, you can make a reasonable copy of some "star" brands. You now also know several techniques for scenting your own talcum powder and bath lotions, so blend away. ❀ YOUR PERFUME WILL TAKE ITS CHARACTER FROM A BLENDING OF HIGH (OR TOP), MIDDLE, AND LOW (OR BASE) NOTES—JUST LIKE MUSIC. The middle notes are principally responsible for the true olfactory flavor of the scent, but you should blend from all three groups to get a balanced fragrance. There are some flower scents, however, that have perfectly balanced high, middle, and low notes of their own: gardenia, tuberose, and lovely lavender are amongst these. Indeed, these flowers are often the single-note inspiration for some famous fragrances: tuberose is the key-note of the perfume Chlöe, and lily-of-the-valley is the heart of Diorissimo.

The high notes ❀ THESE VANISH FAIRLY QUICKLY, BUT GIVE THE FIRST BURST

OF SCENT. Experiment with basil, bergamot, cardamom, coriander, hyacinth, lemon, lemon grass, lime, mint, orange, petitgrain, pine, strawberry, and tarragon.

The middle notes ❀ THESE GIVE YOUR FRAGRANCE ITS CHARACTERISTIC

SCENT AND WILL LAST MANY HOURS—usually from one to two days. Use the blends with care. You might find it works best to play around one main note or you may try to find a floral bouquet. Experiment with black pepper, cypress, galbanum, gardenia, geranium, ginger, honeysuckle, jasmine, lavender, marjoram, mimosa, neroli (orange blossom), nutmeg, peony, rose, rosemary, tea tree, thyme, tuberose, violet, and ylang-ylang.

The low notes ❀ THESE HAVE A CALMING EFFECT AND HAVE THE QUALITY

OF FIXING YOUR FRAGRANCE. They will last for a few days and add a creamy richness to your fragrance. Most are derived from wood oils and are familiar in incense sticks: benzoin, cedar, cinnamon, frankincense, myrrh, oakmoss, patchouli, sandalwood, vanilla, vetiver.

The blend ❀ ALWAYS LABEL YOUR BLENDS CAREFULLY, NOTING THE NUMBER OF

DROPS YOU USE. Use a good-quality bottle with a firm stopper, and leave your mixture to steep for a day or two before smelling again to see what you have created.

Scent families ✿ THE FAMILIES OF SCENT YOU WILL BE MOST FAMILIAR WITH WORK AROUND SEVERAL CENTRAL BOUQUETS. Aldehydes are the most famous floral French fragrances, and they amplify the top notes alongside the middle notes. They are usually floral bouquets and include the rose and jasmine heart of Joy, which is also present in Chanel No. 5. ✿ THE GREEN FLORALS ARE INSTANTLY IDENTIFIABLE, REMINDING US OF GREEN GRASS AND EARLY SPRING. Vetiver is usually a central note in these bouquets, which include Balmain's Ivoire and Armani's Gio. The fruity florals have a high note of strawberry or a base note like vanilla to give the characteristic scent: Elizabeth Arden's Sunflowers, and Calvin Klein's Escape come into this category. Fresh florals center on citrus, or very light floral notes—Anaïs Anaïs is a wonderful example, while woody florals amplify the woody base notes— think of Safari by Ralph Lauren, or Lauder's White Linen. The sweet florals are among the most distinctive: Arden's Blue Grass is the original; Annick Goutal's Gardenia Passion is a more recent example. ✿ ORIENTALS CAN BE SPICY, BUT THEY CAN ALSO BE QUITE FLOWERY—THE LATTER ARE CALLED "FLORIENTALS." If these are your favorites, you are drawn to the voluptuous, musky scents—they are also more aphrodisiac than the lighter florals. The group is typified by Guerlain's Samsara or Yves Saint Laurent's Opium. The florientals are both powerful and flowery, and mix spices with the flowers: Spellbound by Lauder is a perfect example, as is Joop. The so-called spicy orientals linger more on the base notes of culinary spices: the vanilla-rich Angel (Mugler) and Comme des Garçons are signature scents in this group. ✿ THERE ARE ALSO FRUITIER ORIENTALS, WHICH COMBINE JASMINE WITH FRUITY NOTES: Casmir by Chopard and Laura Biagiotti's Roma illustrate this group. The animal orientals, which have a leathery

kind of heart, include Calvin Klein's Obsession, which has amber as a key note. Donna Karan is also an oriental, but a "sweet oriental." ✿ CHYPRES SCENTS EMPHASIZE THE LOVELY NOTES OF BERGAMOT AND MOSSY LOW NOTES: YOU CAN SMELL THE RESINS IN THE BASE. Miss Dior and Paloma Picasso's signature fragrance are perfect examples. A more floral chypres—where the floral note is balanced with the undernotes—would be Montana. A fruity chypres plays on the fruity high notes: Yves Saint Laurent's Champagne is a classic. ✿ IF YOU WANT TO PLAY AROUND WITH THE NEWEST FRAGRANCE FAMILY, YOU MIGHT TRY AN "OCEANIC" OR "OZONIC" FRAGRANCE. These are designed to include a fantasy note—of water or air, or even algae or sea-moss. Base notes are oakmoss or labdanum, and there is a very light floral overlay. Eau d'Issey is one of the best-known ozonics. ✿ REMEMBER TO APPLY YOUR PERFUME ELIXIR TO YOUR PULSE POINTS, THE BACK OF THE NECK, OR BEHIND THE EARS, FOR MAXIMUM EROTIC EFFECT. Your scent will keep longer in a dark bottle, and you should use up your creations reasonably quickly: any scent (including the commercial variety) has a limited life span once it has been opened.

Tricks to play with your signature scent

❀ SCENT LINGERIE. Use sheets of brown paper scented lightly with your chosen fragrance. You can also put cotton balls into an underwear drawer, impregnated with a few drops of the oils that characterize your fragrance. To be more aesthetic, use blotting paper and cotton cosmetic pads cut into shapes and dipped in scent, then tucked into pretty muslin bags and tied with colored ribbons.

❀ SCENT YOUR CROWNING GLORY. Nothing is more seductive than fragrant tresses of wonderfully clean hair. Find a glass bottle into which you can decant some good-quality spring water and the recipe for your signature scent—just the main oils. When your hair is still damp from post-conditioning or when you want to add style each day, spritz a little of this fragrant water into your hair and leave to dry as naturally as possible. Perfume is especially effective in the hair, where it lasts longest. Avoid putting undiluted oils straight onto your scalp, however.

❀ SCENT THE FURNITURE. Place muslin bags filled with cotton cosmetic pads and cotton balls that have been steeped with your favorite scent behind the big cushions in your living room or even inside cushions that zip open. When they are leaned upon they will release your special fragrance, and your whole home will start to take on a signature scent of you.

❀ SCENT YOUR OFFICE. Tie ribbons around files and bunches of pencils, spraying the ribbon first to impregnate it with the smell. Add a cushion to your work chair, and either treat it with a ribbon tied around it (ribbons always add magic and work spells on everyday objects), or fill it with potpourri and scent. You will offset impersonal smells in the workspace and soon stamp your own personality on the environment.

✿ SCENT YOUR OWN SOAP. Scented soap is often the most expensive luxury, but you can create your own by saturating muslin in your signature scent and then wrapping the muslin around an unscented cake of soap. Tie it into a dark plastic bag for a few weeks. You will then have a delightful bath or hand-basin treat that will send out your bewitching scent everywhere.

✿ SCENT CANDLES. These can be used everywhere. Simply burn a candle for a few minutes until the wax has softened at the top. Blow it out, and then add a few drops of your chosen oil/fragrance to the melted wax. Let it harden again, and when you light it after a few minutes, it will dispense your fragrance.

✿ NEVER DO ALL OF THE ABOVE AT THE SAME TIME. Overkill is the least seductive thing in the world of scent as in anything else. Step lightly.

Suppliers

ALEXANDER ESSENTIALS
P.O. Box 11709,
London SE14 5ZR
Tel: 020 7732 8686
www.alexander-essentials.com
Essential oils and other aromatherapy products including powdered damiana.

THE AROMATIC COMPANY
LINCS Aromatic Ltd,
Unit 18,
Thames Street, Louth,
Lincs. LN11 7AD
Tel: 0800 996 1148
www.aromatic.co.uk
A wide variety of essential oils.

CULPEPER LTD
Hadstock Road, Linton,
Cambridge CB1 6NJ
Tel: 01223 894054
www.culpeper.com
Dried herbs, pot pourri and oils.

JEKKA HERB FARM
Rose Cottage,
Shellards Lane, Alveston,
Bristol BS35 3SY
Tel: 01454 418878
www.jekka.co.uk
Fresh herbs in pots, and seeds.

KOBASHI ESSENTIAL OILS
2 Fore Street,
Ide, Devon EX2 9RQ
Tel: 01392 217628
www.kobashi.com
A range of essential oils.

MEADOWSWEET OILS
18 Dalston Gardens,
Off Honeypot Lane,
Stanmore,
Middlesex HA7 1BU
Tel: 020 8204 4441
www.meadowsweet.co.uk
A varied range of essential oils.

MEDICHEST.COM ONLINE DRUGSTORE
Tel: 1-800-714-8875
www.medichest.com
Hard-to-find personal care products, including ethyl alcohol.

NEAL'S YARD REMEDIES
Head Office:
26-34 Ingate Place, Battersea
London SW8 3NS
Tel: 020 7498 1686
www.nealsyardremedies.com

Mail Order:
29 John Dalton Street,
Manchester M2 6DS
Tel: 0161 831 7875
*A full range of dried herbs and
essential oils.*

Simplers Botanical Company
P.O. Box 39,
Forestville, CA 95436-0039
Tel: 1-800-652-7646
www.simplers.com
Organic essential oils.

Space NK Apothecary Ltd
Head Office:
200 Great Portland Street,
London W1W 5QG
Tel: 020 7299 4999
www.spacenk.co.uk

Mail Order:
Tel: 0870 169 9999
Pheremone and a range of perfumes.

Star Child
2-4 The High Street,
Glastonbury,
Somerset BA6 9DU
Tel: 01458 834663
www.starchild.co.uk
*Dried herbs, essential and perfume
oils and incense.*

Tisserand Aromatherapy
Newtown Road, Hove,
East Sussex BN3 7BA
Tel: 01273 325666
www.tisserand.com
A wide range of essential oils.

Index

Acknowledgments

Author's acknowledgments

Too many to mention: I have learned so much from so many generous-hearted people across the globe. However, meeting Anthony Dweck at Harrods three years ago has left a wonderful legacy; also Roger Phillips and Nicky Foy, whose *Herbs* is one of the best reference books of many that I have. Thanks, too, to Candace Bahouth — a love potion entirely in human form — and her sage husband, Andrew; to Saris and Astrid, who imparted some ideas along these lines years ago; to Jan de Vries and Lesley Bremness, who know more about herbs, I think, than anyone breathing; and to the local brewers of lots of herbal tonics in my native Somerset. Special thanks to P, not just for ideas and faith in me, but also, very recently, for the gift of African spices she produced for sampling. To Anne, Jim, and Alison, for dedication and professionalism. And if your name belongs here but cannot appear because of space, yet you know who you are, have thanks from me for so, so much edification and joy. Blessed be.

Published by Cedco Publishing in 2002

100 Pelican Way, San Rafael, CA 94901
www.cedco.com

First published in 2002 by Quadrille Publishing Ltd,
Alhambra House, 27-31 Charing Cross Road, London wc2h 0ls

Publishing Director Anne Furniss
Design Jim Smith
Editorial Assistant Katie Ginn
Production Nancy Roberts

© Text Titania Hardie 2002
© Photographs Sara Morris 2002
© Layout and design Quadrille Publishing Ltd 2002

isbn 0-7683-2497-1
Printed and bound in China

92